RYAN'S WO[RLD]

The Voice of a Pree[mie]
"Query"
November 1, 2010

I would like to introduce you to my second book, my first non-fiction, "Ryan's World". The book, a completed 22,000-word biography, is one of many untold stories of events, tribulations, faiths and strengths influencing the determination of a premature baby with little hope of survival.

The book begins with the voice of a premature embryo speaking from the womb. The story chronicles events, consequences, results and outcomes of the unexpected. This is a book with a purpose, written to instill a promise of hope to families struggling with disabilities and targeted to a society influenced by feeling, sympathy and curiosity.

Faiths and strengths from family members influencing and becoming influenced by the birth and development of a special needs little girl, following her through a journey of life, are told through photographs and special accounts supporting a particular purpose, giving significance to the spirit of a challenged life.

Inspiration comes from the knowledge of countless children born too soon for their families to expect help through support organizations. It comes from knowledge of cruelty in an uneducated society many decades ago, looking upon the special needs members of our communities as wasted and unwanted, forcing them to live in institutions. Inspiration comes from the work of Eunice Kennedy Schriver, realizing the compassion and conscious emotion of the special needs, and working to provide training and sports through the Special Olympics.

Written to instill a promise of hope for families having experienced the initial overwhelming shock of hearing their child has developmental disabilities, *"Ryan's World"* means to give support through the toughest of times. The book, meant to give a spirit of compassion and optimism to the disabled reminds them of incredible opportunities available to make a difference in a life once thought of as unessential.

The book, written by one, who has shared the anxiety and heartache, and importance of belonging in the world of a family member with a particular purpose, bringing delight, joy and happiness, is an inspirational vision of life's significance in a world of tumult.

For those, accepting a penalty of punishment; a quote from (Shakespeare) *'Tis most strange Nature should be so conversant with pain."*

RYAN'S WORLD

THE VOICE OF A PREEMIE

BARBARA SULLIVAN NELSON

WESTBOW
PRESS
A DIVISION OF THOMAS NELSON

WestBow Press books may be ordered through booksellers or by contacting:

WestBow Press
A Division of Thomas Nelson
1663 Liberty Drive
Bloomington, IN 47403
www.westbowpress.com
1-(866) 928-1240

Because of the dynamic nature of the Internet, any Web addresses or links contained in this book may have changed since publication and may no longer be valid. The views expressed in this work are solely those of the author and do not necessarily reflect the views of the publisher, and the publisher hereby disclaims any responsibility for them.

Any people depicted in stock imagery provided by Thinkstock are models, and such images are being used for illustrative purposes only.

Certain stock imagery © Thinkstock.

ISBN: 978-1-4497-1105-4 (sc)
ISBN: 978-1-4497-1106-1 (e)

Library of Congress Control Number: 2011920783

Printed in the United States of America

WestBow Press rev. date: 3/2/2011

RYAN'S WORLD

(The Voice of a Preemie)

"No! No! Not yet. I'm not ready. I'm not big enough. My mommy isn't ready. What are they saying? What does emergency mean? I need to grow more. I'm not strong enough to live in the outside. I need the protection of my Mommy. I want to hear and see the world. I want to talk and walk. Twenty-six weeks in the dark gave me an opportunity to collect many thoughts. I have plenty to say.

Where are they taking my mommy and me? What hospital is better for me than the one here? What is cesarean surgery? We arrive at Norton's Children's Hospital. Everyone is excited, running around as if in a big hurry. "Hey out there, what's the big rush?" My parents and grandparents are here. My aunt Sharon got all panicky and called my grandmother home from her trip... Some more of my aunts are here. They look sad. My dad is nervous but my mommy is calm. I wonder what they gave her. They are talking about her blood pressure. I hope she is ok; she is trying hard to protect me. I am feeling very tired. It is hard to move around.

More doctors and nurses are coming in. They have masks on their faces. They are not talking a lot. Why are they washing their hands so hard? They must really be dirty.

Oh! Oh! They look worried. They are worried about my mommy and me too. Please, if it will help my mommy to get better I will come out now. What are they doing? The doctor is cutting my mommy. "Hey you, don't hurt my mommy. Why can't they hear me?" Someone is picking me up. I feel cold air and there are bright lights everywhere.

Everyone is rushing around. The nurse is holding me. Where are you taking me?

She is putting me on a scale. I want to go back with my mommy where it is warm and I feel safe. "What? One pound and how many ounces; that is pretty scrawny." They are taking their time cleaning me up. Are they afraid I will break? Now the nurse is putting me in a glass cage. I feel warm and very tired. It is hard to breathe. I have no clothes on. People are staring at me and I am "butt naked". Where are my fingernails and toenails? I don't have hair. Why did my dad faint when he looked at me? Two people in green space suits are picking him up off the floor. If I can just get them to hear me, hey out there; don't let my dad get hurt. It's bad enough that my mommy and I are having a difficult time." I can't cry with this tube down my throat. How can I eat or take a bottle? How will I grow without food? "Ouch! They are sticking me with needles and putting tubes in my arms."

A MOTHER'S FEAR, A GRANDMOTHER'S ANGUISH

"It is March 15, 1983, a significant date, as March 15 is my own Grandmother's birthday. Authentic as her name, Grandma Jones, the matriarch of a large family, including 11 children, lived until the age of 93. She remains a special remembrance in the lives of all her descendants. I cannot help but think how proud she would be to have a great, great grandchild born on her special day.

My flight touched down at Louisville's International Airport, and my middle daughter, Sharon, met me at the arrival gate. The expression on her face confirmed fearful concerns, causing my knees to weaken and body to tremble.

It is five days before her 25th birthday and the life of my youngest daughter, Janet, is at risk. Forced into labor by an unknown virus after only 26 weeks of pregnancy, an ambulance rushed my funny, smart, beautiful little girl, the always-available person for the entire family to rely on, from one hospital to another one, better equipped for premature deliveries. Admitted to Norton's Hospital for a delivery to save her unborn child, my daughter's blood pressure is dangerously low. Emotions reflected by the pounding of my heart are ungovernable.

With your child experiencing a difficult labor, the recognition of Motherhood becomes a conscious awareness beyond the laws of nature. Bargaining with God becomes the ultimate goal.

The family support for one another and the faith and prayers of everyone anxiously concerned, provides a providence of strength directed through the Heavens, and rewards an injured family a prayer answered. A fragile baby girl, delicately lifted from the womb as her mother's vital signs begin to improve, gives evidence of God's influence on the breath of life and soul of man. Awareness of serious obstacles, challenging threats of complications to such a small infant, remains unsaid.

RYAN

"I have been in this glass display case for several days now. My mommy looks better but she is worried about me. I can tell. They talk about my mommy going home from the hospital. How can that be? She is always here. My dad is always here. I guess he got over his fainting spell. Could have been something he ate."

The days have turned into weeks since Janet's health returned to a healthier, sound condition. Our prayers centered on my tiny little granddaughter, Ryan.

It is early afternoon in April of 1983, when the sunshine, overshadowed by an urgent summons for the family, dims pleasures of welcome to our family's littlest miracle.

Ryan's heart is repeatedly stopping; she is bleeding through every opening in her frail body. It is time to say goodbye. The pain of realization is unbearable... At my family's insistence, I stayed home while other family members remained at the hospital to comfort parents choosing not to put their little one through more agonizing pain. The dialysis machine is disconnected. Ryan is administered the sacrament of Holy Baptism by Reverend Myers, the Hospital Chaplain, on April 2, 1983. She is 18 days old.

"The nurses and doctors talk about me a lot. They are always around. Just when I start feeling better, they poke me with another needle. I hear them say things like, "she has an open blood vessel in her heart and a third of her weight is fluid." "Do they think I can't hear? I want to shout, Get over it and fix it. It doesn't matter what's wrong if it's fixable. So what if my kidneys failed. Get on with the dialysis. I can

take it. The chaplain is talking to my parents and now she is pouring water over my bald head. I'm very little to be baptized.

Ok, now what? Blood is coming through my nose, ears, eyes and everywhere. My heart stopped three times today. I hear them talk about it but it's my heart. I know when it stops. I just have to start it again. They asked my mommy if she wants to hold me for the first time. Why is she crying? I am not ready to say goodbye. This is what I have been waiting for. I want to feel my mommy again. We have conquered many obstacles and they haven't seen anything yet. Everyone has left the room. I heard my parents say they will be in the waiting room. I know they are sad. I have to help them."

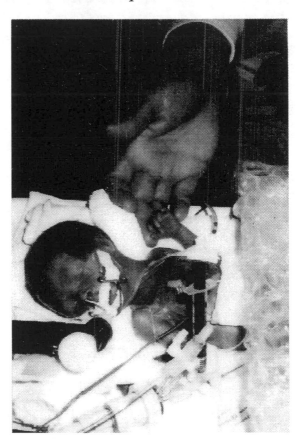

A FATHER'S COMMITMENT

Steven Moss

March 15, 1983. The first day of a new life. The first day of a journey. The new life for Ryan Moss will have unforeseen and far reaching effects on everyone in her family.

The journey starts with my visit to the intensive care third floor of Kosair Children's Hospital to see my newborn daughter. I almost fainted. The nurse was using a long plastic tube to suck mucous from her nose and throat. A respirator drew her every breath. The nurse tried to explain what was happening.

Ryan, born 14 weeks early, required such a vast array of tubes, monitors, tests, machines and medical staff to support her life that it was not understandable at first. During the five months after her birth, Ryan lived in the hospital. During this period, my knowledge of medicine and the delicate balance in the human body grew immensely.

Months of daily visits, dozens of surgeries, and meetings with specialized doctors who I never knew existed, all play their part in the journey that was to last the rest of my life and change the path of my life in ways I could never imagine.

Ryan has beaten all the predictions we were given about her abilities. Doctors first told us she would never walk, never talk, never see, and on and on. Ryan's disabilities prevent her from living a life that most people would consider normal. Ryan has simple desires, wanting no more than she has.

Ryan is mentally challenged, has cerebral palsy, is legally blind, speaks in a way that many can't understand and a hundred other things which many of us would consider serious enough to make us feel sorry for ourselves. But, Ryan wakes up every day singing. Her life is wonderful. Most of us could benefit from her outlook on life to make our lives joyful.

If you're paying attention, by now you will have guessed the lives of her parents is much more difficult than hers. Facing these difficulties on a daily basis can motivate you to find a better way.

Sometime around 1990, I had a series of dreams. I had no idea how these dreams would materialize, how much I would learn, how much I would grow, and the possibilities that would present themselves to me.

My dream was about Ryan's future. I had passed on and Ryan was living in a place that was safe, happy and productive. When I awakened the next day, I started planning how I would be able to create this place. Through my efforts and investigation, I was given the name of a woman who had started a group called "Apple Patch" I met with this group of mothers of children with disabilities. It seems this group had the same vision I had.

The mothers all had the best intentions, but at the rate they were going, we would be lucky if the dreams were realized in my lifetime. So, I joined up. We attracted new members, formed a board of directors, formed a 501c non-profit and, before I knew it, I was chairman.

My first major task was to raise money. We found a sponsor and held the first fundraising event, "The Apple Patch 5K run in 1990. $40,000.00 was the income. We were on our way.

Years of fundraising, meetings and learning convinced me that we needed to take the next step and hire our first employee. It was a battle for me to convince all the tightwad mothers to make the commitment, but it happened.

This was the first milestone for "Apple Patch". We would shortly be seen as a viable organization and be taken seriously by many members of the community. Within a few short months we had three staff, a donated office in a church and the interest of some folks that would make a difference.

The first was Frank Otte. Frank and Peggy Otte have a son with Down's syndrome. The couple developed a special interest in what "Apple Patch" was doing. Ultimately , Frank and Peggy donated 50 acres in Brownsboro KY at exit 14 on 1-71. This was the second milestone for "Apple Patch"

As we prepared to design the place we all had wanted, there was as much turmoil as progress. The type of community we all had dreamed of, a closed, private cluster of group homes, was no longer embraced by the agencies and organizations which will guide the best practices for the way adults with disabilities are treated.

So, after designing the entire 50 acre site and construction on the first group home, we were experiencing a difficult financial period. The board of directors asked the executive director to resign and started a search for a new leader.

With the hiring of Chris Stevenson, we found exactly what we needed. Chris's vision and leadership changed the face of "Apple Patch" immensely. Today, "Apple Patch" operates five staffed residences providing residential supports for 60 adults with disabilities. An extensive day program provides therapeutic and recreational services for 90 individuals. "Apple Patch" has an annual budget approaching six million dollars and continues to grow.

RYAN

"It is morning again. My glass bed is against the wall in the corner of the room. The nurse is coming over. She has a white sheet in her hand. What does she plan to do with that? She certainly got excited when I showed her that I could stop bleeding and operate my own kidneys without a machine. "Wow, I guess I did show her something. Everyone is running into the room. They are smiling and laughing at me and at each other. I heard a nurse say; "I didn't expect her to live through the night, I came in the early morning and didn't recognize her." "Everyone is hugging. Both my parents are smiling. I love it when everyone is happy. I am a little tired now; hey out there, if you are going to have a party, wait until I get bigger and get out of this see-through basket."

Gradually, Ryan gained enough weight to be transferred into an Annex at the Hospital, A closer step home from 3M. This is a step up for premature infants. She slowly began to improve. After coming off the breathing machine, the next achievement, for Ryan, was learning how to eat from a nipple. Janet remembers the special attention from the nurses and staff. Several made gifts for the small baby and one nurse brought her a doll from Germany.

Ryan is still remembered for her size of just over a pound at birth, and especially for her determination in clinging to life. Along with her sweetness and fine qualities, her strong will and doggedness remains a special attribute.

"I'm a little older now and getting bigger. The nurses and friends of my Meemaw started making clothes for me out of napkins. It's about time. I am tired of showing my private areas to every Tom, Dick and who knows glaring through the window. My parents can hold me in the rocker when they visit. Sometimes they both come in during the night.

They just stand there and stare at me. They always have masks on their faces but I know when they are here. It's good to see them; it makes me happy, but give me a break; I need my rest. I'm sure they need theirs.

The doctors told my parents that I would never walk or talk. They don't expect me to know much either. My mommy spends every day in the chapel. They tell me she is praying for the doctors to be wrong on this one."

THE FACTS

Taken from "Interviews" Norton Kosair-
Children's Hospital (Vol. 8, Number 3)
Fall 1983 **"Against odds that nobody thought she could**
beat, tiny Ryan Moss, lived, a testimony to the care
in the neonatal intensive care nursery (3M) in
Kosair-Children's Hospital."

This baby survived against all odds because of the doctors and nurses dedicated to a profession where miracles happen and due to the love of parents, Steve and Janet, who were not willing to give her up, and by Ryan's tenacity in clinging to life. Three months premature, Ryan's birth certificate affirms her to be 12 ½ inches long. Her weight is just over one pound, her legs the size of her mother's smallest finger, her head no bigger than a tangerine and her little feet, the size of her mother's thumb. A respirator assists breathing for lungs too immature to inhale.

The day after Ryan's birth, having met her daughter for the first time, Janet signed surgery papers for doctors to close a blood vessel in the tiny baby's heart. "A patent ductus arteriosis, a blood vessel in the heart often does not close after birth in premature babies." When Ryan was 26 days old, her kidneys failed. Bloated, swollen and hemorrhaging, she developed "bronchopulmonary displasia" or scarred lungs, a common occurrence in premature babies on respirators. After 24 hours on dialysis, a third of her weight fluid, doctors prepared Steve and Janet for a heart wrenching decision. The baby's size hindered chances of survival through further procedures. "Nothing else can be done!" Janet held her baby for the first time and what she tearfully prepared for the last time. The nurses were fighting back tears. The baby's heart stopped three times that day. Each time her heart stopped, Ryan was handed to her mother to hold. No one expected the baby to live through the night except her father, Steve, who kept saying, "She is going to be fine." It is a long night. Ryan's parents keep vigil at the hospital. They are unable to sleep, aware the precious time for their baby daughter to be a part of their family is ending.

The next morning, a nurse went to Ryan's small crib. To her amazement upon feeling the damp sheet under the small infant, she discovered the baby's kidneys working. The doctors and nurses coming in on the morning shift didn't recognize her. One doctor commented. "Absolutely remarkable"! The hospital staff joined the parents in anticipation of a feeling of hope.

The elation was short lived. Ryan developed another obstacle of extreme. She began to bleed into her brain. Tubes or shunts inserted to drain off fluids relieved the problem, only to be followed by the discovery of a cyst in her brain. Ryan's parents were not daunted. Janet exclaimed, "She's too spunky to let a little old cyst get her down". The cyst may eventually cause Ryan developmental problems. "A follow-up program to monitor the baby's development can plug her in early into infant stimulation programs if necessary for special attention" offers the neonatology physician, "it was such a triumph for all of us when Ryan came off the breathing machine."

Janet and Steve enrolled in CPR classes, learning resuscitation techniques and preparing to take their small baby, four months and 22 days old home. "Around midnight, the first night Ryan was home, the Moss family got a phone call. It was Ryan's nurses from 3M checking up on their little miracle baby."

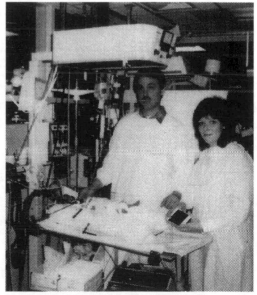

Steven and Janet checking up on their little one

RECOLLECTIONS BY A GRANDFATHER

Don Butts

As I sit in the hospital hour after hour praying for Janet, my youngest daughter and her baby, Ryan, I look at the smallest baby I have ever seen and feel her spirit and her little voice speaking to me.

"My baby's butt is dirty, I heard my mommy say." "Make yourself useful" said the nurse, handing her a cotton ball. Most kids my age are getting their butts wiped with a warm, soft, moist cloth and sprinkled with delicate aromatic powder. Me, I get a quick wipe with a cotton ball. Then these pampered kids get a warm, snug, contoured diaper tucked around them. Me, they raise me up and slap another flat pad underneath my body. I'll get even someday, when I take my diaper off and run out the door au naturel. This is all very humiliating to me while I lie here stark naked in front of strangers, all spread eagle, centerfold fashion. It's bad enough in front of parents and grandparents but in front of other relatives and doctors, nurses and even strangers gawking through the glass window. I'll get even some day when I am a teenager and want to wear skimpy clothes. I'm a bit too little now to be concerned with modesty. I can't even reach down and pull a cover over myself. When they do cover me, it's with a piece of plastic with air pockets.

"My relatives aren't all teary eyed when they visit now. I am four months old. I don't weigh much but it is very different from just over a pound.

Finally, the day is here. I am with my parents and the hovering attention that will prove to be mine forever. I am four months and 22 days old and looking forward to having my own room. I like my room. The walls, painted a pale color, have pink and blue elephants. Elephants are supposed to bring good luck. My bed is pretty and cozy. It is a lot bigger than the bed in the hospital. I wonder who will use that bed now. I will pray for them to get better like me.

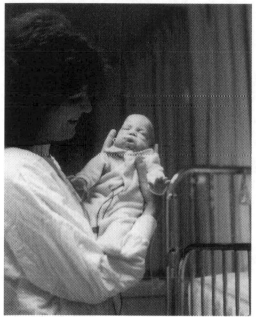

Neonatal Unit, preparing to go home.

In my new room at home there are things bouncing over my bed to look at. A lamp sings me to sleep. Sometimes when I awaken, I make noises when I get lonely to see my mom and dad. They rush into my room when they hear a sound. I could almost laugh aloud.

I get dressed up in pretty clothes often, even when we don't have company or go anywhere. Many people visit, usually Grandparents gushing and talking baby talk to me. My aunts, uncles, and my parent's friends bring gifts, mostly clothes. They must have felt sorry for me at the hospital when everyone stared at my naked body. They called it the "Neonatal Unit". It should have been called the "Naked Navel Unit". I like it when my cousins visit. There are a lot of them and they are all bigger than I am.

It's hard to sleep with all that light shining through my window. I think my parents have figured that out. They are hanging blankets at the window. Finally, I get to sleep longer. I am probably not the only one thankful for that.

My Dad gets up early; sometimes it is still dark outside. He goes to work most days; I'm not sure what that means but I like it when he comes back. My Mom stays home with me until time to take me to the doctor. There are many doctors out there. I think she wants to visit all of them. I wonder how long that will take.

I am eating big food now, not just drinking milk. My Grandmother Mary makes baby food from garden vegetables. It is cozy when someone holds me and feeds me. I like it when they rock me in the big rocker and play music or sing. My mom and dad play music for me all the time. I wish I could tell them how much I like it. Someday I will let them know. It will be interesting to get to know all my relatives and to hear what they think of me. Being so small and all."

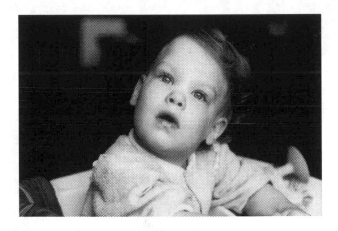

AUGUST 28, 1983

A Grandmother's Thanks
As Printed in the Courier Journal, Louisville, KY

A special recognition for those attending physicians, for the staff members on 3M at Kosair-Children's Hospital, and for the work carried on from donations made by supporters of Louisville's Crusade for Children.

On March 15, Janet and Stephen Moss rushed to Norton Hospital for the arrival of their three-month-premature baby. The quick decision was made by Janet's physician, who knew the unborn infant would require specialized care and equipment just to survive the initial shock of the outside world. At 5:15 p.m., a daughter, Ryan Leslie Moss, was born, weighing one pound six and one-half ounces. The smallest baby that Dr. John Farmer had ever dreamed of delivering had but a small chance of survival.

Tiny Ryan…was immediately handed over to the highly trained team of physicians and nurses on the staff at Kosair-Children's Hospital…. The delicate little girl was placed on life-support systems, which had largely been donated to the hospital by Louisville's Crusade for Children.

The dedication and care that little Ryan was to receive in the months that followed far exceeded the routine duties of the staff on 3M. It seemed to the family that almost every complication that could happen to such a premature baby did, in fact, happen. When Ryan was but a few hours old, she was taken to surgery to have a valve closed in her heart. On April 7, she required thoracic duct surgery; and on April 15, at one month old, she underwent a kidney dialysis, which was performed as a desperate attempt to save her life.

Ryan had suffered a stroke, kidney failure, and was hemorrhaging internally. It was at this moment Janet held her baby for the first time, and what she and Stephen feared could be the last time. Soon the baby's reflexes improved enough to chance the kidney dialysis, which she miraculously survived. When she weighed a healthier three pounds, a shunt was implanted under the skin in her temple to prevent fluid retention, which could cause permanent damage.

After four months and 22 days in the hospital, most of which was spent in 3M's intensive care unit at Kosair-Children's Hospital, Ryan went home to live a normal life with her anxious parents. What wonderfully special challenge has God prepared for Ryan, to have labored through the hands of all these skilled, dedicated and loving people to spare my beautiful little granddaughter?

"Barbara L. Nelson"

A HOSPITAL MEETING GOALS THROUGH CAMPAIGNING FOR DONATIONS

www.kosair.com/shrinerscharities.html

The Kosair Shrine Temple and Kosair Charities Committee, Inc. support the medical care of children. The members serve on the Board of the Shriners Hospital's for Children.

Their volunteers transport children in local areas as well as provide hundreds of thousands of dollars to hospitals in support of local and National systems. They use their talents, time and energies continuing the legacy of love and compassion affecting the lives of countless children and their families. "Each member of Kosair Shrine Temple is also a member of Kosair Charities Committee, Inc. Thus, each Kosair Shriner can be proud of the Medical Miracles that occur daily in the hospital." In 1926 Kosair Shrine Temple opened its own free hospital for crippled children. "By the 1980's the medical needs of children had changed. The Board of directors of Kosair Charities Committee, Inc. acted on the advice of the medical community to combine medical services with another hospital to provide a more full range of care for the children. The other Hospital was Children's Hospital, a part of what was then known as Norton Infirmary."

A new entity was created named Kosair Children's Hospital in Louisville, KY which opened in 1986. It is an affiliate of Kosair Shrine Temple owned by Norton Healthcare. Financial support from Kosair Charities, supplemented by large donations by businesses and individuals, are key factors in renovation, expansion, recruitment of healthcare workers and continuing research programs. Norton Healthcare has the responsibility of operation. An effort to compete with hospitals in other cities requires a constant community effort. The importance of taking care of society's most vulnerable children becomes a responsibility of all involved citizens.

Many untold stories lie hidden within the walls of Kosair Children's Hospital and the Shriners Hospitals for children throughout the nation. Some are more challenging than others but all-important to the patients, their families and the dedicated health care workers having experienced the care and love provided by a growing facility and caring community.

Ryan's Uncle Guy is the first person in our family to experience help and support through the Kosair Charities. My brother was admitted to the Kosair Crippled Children's hospital on Eastern Parkway in the late 1940's, when a young boy. He underwent surgery to correct a bone crippling disease identified as Perthes disease. A rare disease of the hip, more common in boys than in girls, Perthes usually affects children between the ages of four and ten. My brother, ignored this as a teenager, and joined the paratroopers. One jump and then the discovery of several steel staples in his leg forced a medical discharge. In later years, my brother, a plumber, became a skilled dance instructor. This gives early value to the work through the Kosair charities.

The story written about Ryan is only one story of a family's love and support, transported to a little girl with not much chance of survival, giving her a determination and will to surpass all odds of failing circumstances and grow to touch the hearts of all who share her life. Although Ryan's skill's are confined and restricted within the limits of underdevelopment, she has far surpassed expectations of skeptical predictions from some physicians who attended her. She proved their efforts not in vain, but a remarkable challenge to a science of medicine and success of wisdom and faith.

Ryan lives in a happy world, all her own, with possession of her own thoughts. She shares a perception and understanding defined in the tender feelings of warmth and affection with everyone. Although having been taught the social graces of society of how to sit like a lady, when to say please and thank you, which she never fails to express, Ryan's skills define tact in a different way. One incident brought to mind by her Mother tells of taking Ryan, as a teenager, to a doctor's office. The doctor turned to walk out of the examining room, when Ryan, evidently not satisfied by his failure to listen, shouts at him,

"Doctor! I am talking to you."

The Doctor gleefully responded to a commanding authority.

Medical technology, combined with Community support continue to provide care and a future for deserving children as Kentucky's only Pediatric Hospital, continues to grow for the many Ryan's, yet to arrive. Today, Ryan's cousin, Lauren, the same age as Ryan, is one of the caregivers in the same neonatal unit that protected and gave life to a little girl once given up for lost.

GRANDMOTHER MARY AND HER SPECIAL GIRL

Mary Moss

The first night Ryan stayed overnight with me when she was so very small I continually checked her breathing as she lay in a small crib next to my bed. We both survived the night, but Ryan was the only one with a good nights sleep. I continually checked to see if she was still breathing.

When she was older, I began a labor of love on my days off from work, making meals for her from fresh vegetables. When she was a little older, I gave her a piece of graham cracker. She looked at it but didn't quite know what to do. I held her hand and put it up to her mouth. After the first taste, she knew exactly what to do. Ryan, to this day, calls every food she eats,

"*my favorite*."

Ryan learned to walk and talk against all predictions of most of her doctors. When she was learning to walk at five years old, she liked to walk in the hall with one hand on the wall and me at her other side. The wall seemed to steady her. I remember her standing by her bed in her room about eight feet from me and, without encouragement or suggestion, she suddenly walked across the room toward me, about 12 steps without support. What a wonderful exciting event for all of us.

The first day she spoke a word is another special memory. After making rolls for dinner, I told her what they were. Later in the day, after seeing them again and without prompting, I heard her say "roll".

After she began walking well, Ryan wasn't quite happy staying away from home overnight. I remember one evening in particular when she was especially difficult about going to bed. She kept asking for her parents, whom she called "Big Car" and

Ryan at five years old.

"Big Truck". She related to her mom, Janet, driving a car while Stephen, her dad, a truck. I didn't rationalize calling her parents in the middle of the night. She didn't stay overnight for several months after that episode.

When she advanced to talking more, it was noticeably frustrating and difficult for her to pronounce some words. Practicing a list of words I prepared for her eventually evolved into writing words and spelling them. We started out with three letter words and have advanced to five letter words. Ryan continues her practice of words with me today and never seems to tire.

A REMINDER OF COMPASSION

It is a challenge for families having children mentally underdeveloped and with physical disabilities never to improve with the increments of time. It can be heart breaking when a mentally challenged child reaches college age, after having graduated from a special high school class, receiving mail inviting him/her to investigate a college of choice and the many bankcard invitations offering lines of credit; it can be challenging and it can be humorous. Accepting compassionate looks from adults and curiosity stares from children is an expected occurrence. "All these special rights are among the privileges of having a special child like Ryan."

The feelings of compassion and love inside her is again evident when Ryan sat on the bed next to her Great Grandmother Pearl in the nursing home, realizing with obvious extra perception, what no one else knew, that her Great Grandmother Pearl would not be with us much longer. Ryan patted and stroked her Great Grandmother's back in a gentle motion, her watchful concern obvious. When "Grandma Pearl" left the world of the living and went to live in Heaven with God, as explained, all Ryan asked her mother was, "Did Grandma Pearl take the *Big Road*"?

Taking the Big Road, explained by Janet, when she and Ryan traveled to Tennessee on a road trip, is the expressway and the way Ryan relates to anyone going on a long trip. As she became older, having experienced a few aging family member's deaths, in Ryan's world, taking "The Big Road" means they aren't coming back.

AUNT SUSAN RECALLS

It is November 2008. My 25 year old niece Ryan, solemnly stood next to her Grandpa Butts in the large room filled with beautiful flowers. She looked into the sweet face of her precious "Memaw" as she lay still in the casket. Ryan may have gone unnoticed with the moment until she broke out in song. She sang clear. She sang loud.

"Fly Away Home."

She sang each verse;

"Fly Away Home", waving her arm in motion as if leading the band. To her, no one else was in the room. She was singing her song for her "Me Maw". As conversations ceased among relatives and friends in mourning, arms began to wrap around backs of one another and heads leaned into shoulders while the voice of an angel finished her last chorus;

"Fly Away Home."

Ryan's Aunt Susan, Janet's older sister, remembers a typical conversation by Mother and Daughter. When Ryan finally returned to the adult day care center, the conversation in the car as her Mother was driving started out with Ryan asking questions as usual:

> *Ryan... "What am I going to wear when I go to Heaven, Mommy?"*
>
> *Janet... "Oh! That will be a while. You don't have to think about that right now."*
>
> *Ryan... "When? When am I going to go to Heaven?"*
>
> *Janet... "Not for a long time."*

> *Ryan... "What are you going to wear, Mommy, when you go to Heaven?"*
>
> *Janet   "Well, I don't plan on going for a long time either."*
>
> *Ryan... "I like what "Memaw" was wearing to go to Heaven." I want to wear my pink shirt like that."*
>
> *Janet... "Ok! That's fine, if you still have it by then."*
>
> *Ryan... "Good, Mommy, good. That's what I'll do. I'll wear that."*

They arrive at Saint Mary's Center, an adult day Care. Sister Regina was sitting with the other students when she saw Ryan walk in. She was so pleased to see Ryan.

> **Sister... *Ryan, Where have you been?"***

Janet quietly told Sister that Ryan's Grandmother had passed away. Sister Regina rose and took Ryan's hand.

> **Sister... *Oh, she went to see Jesus?"***
>
> ***Ryan*..**loudly blurted. ***"Yes! It was her special day."***

DECISION DEVELOPMENT

It is Tuesday, September 30, 1997. This evening I arrived at an Elementary School where Ryan is enrolled through CEP, Child Enrichment Program, sponsored by the YMCA, at 5:45 pm, prepared to take Ryan to dinner and have our special time together. As always, after I pick my Granddaughter up, we stop by my house for a last minute grooming and visit to the bathroom. She is always excited to see me; and eager for her grandfather, "Popsie", to join us for her "special night out". Ryan needs help only with her hair and occasionally tucking in her shirt. She is being taught in school and by her parents to conquer disabling deprivation and increase the powers of ability. Because of this, her freedom of control widens the gap from the help and support from others. Her self-reliance continually improves as she gains confidence and independent freedom through the influence of her caretakers. She learns to make minute decisions and graduates to higher levels of decision-making.

I asked Ryan if she preferred spaghetti at Olive Garden, burritos at Tumbleweed or Chinese at Sichuan Gardens. With her sparkling blue eyes darting back and forth and, as she has the last few times, she chose Chinese. Ryan is a creature of familiarity. Next time we visit another restaurant, she will hold on to that idea for several visits. However, she is learning the names of each restaurant and the menus. She never forgets what she ate the time before and continues with her menu of won ton soup, chicken and broccoli, steamed rice, followed by orange sherbet and, "don't forget the fortune cookie". After needing a little help cutting up her broccoli, Ryan ate everything on her plate, as usual, before asking for dessert. She refers to all desserts as "cake/pie". Her good manners at dinner prompted sensibility of my own. Unlike me, Ryan seldom drops a morsel on the table and almost never soils her clothes at mealtime. Each food is her favorite. Of course, like the rest of the family, she does pick out the decadent chocolate dessert when offered a choice.

Ryan, at fourteen years old, continues to be inquisitive and continually asks questions such as;

"Where are we going?

What are we going to do after that?

What are we going to eat next time?

What time does my Mommy get home?

Where is my Popsie?

Why is he playing cards?"

One question after another and she is always satisfied with the answer. She may ask repeat questions in five minutes, but shows an effort of concentration and reasoning. She accepts the answer and promptly awaits an answer to her next question.

Tuesday, October 7, 1997, Ryan and I went to "Happy House," a day care, to pick up her cousin, Ellery, before going home to have chicken strip dinners from Colonel Sanders. Besides placing a lot of emphasis on food, Ryan enjoys interacting with younger cousins and other children. She learns from them and they, in turn, learn how to interact with better understanding the characteristics of special needs.

IN RYAN'S WORLD

Ryan's world is waking up every morning singing; she sings at least three verses of Happy Birthday over the phone to everyone in the family on their special day. She listens to music and dances around the kitchen daily. Her delightful personality obvious to all who have met her, to her friends at the adult daycare center where she spends weekdays and to those in her family, is a welcome diversion from the negative woes of the world.

The many hearts Ryan has touched over the years is a deserving reward that one will not forget. If you feel unloved, she will extend her love to you with a reminder briefly forgotten. If you are sick, she will attempt to make you feel better. If you are sad, she will comfort you. If you forget, she will remind you. Ryan is a special person in her special world, a special person filling a gap in many lives in a world not clearly defined to her. She is a window of happiness and a reminder of importance. The occasional humor found in her childlike truth is undeniably refreshing. The ability of showing her amusing side is a quality she displays in uncontrollable laughter.

Ryan's life, like so many others born with or developing to limited extents, is not in vain. Their lives are not despairing; they are set apart for special reasons. They remind us of the delicate nature of existence, the importance and values of natural feelings, ultimately the acceptance of a divine presence. They are gifts, treasures of inspiration. They are God's influence on a Divine Soul.

GRANDFATHER'S TOUCHING MOMENT

Don Butts

It is June 16, 1983. I am sitting in a rocker in the 3-M unit of Norton's-Children's Hospital holding my 13-week-old granddaughter, a privilege with slim possibilities in the previous weeks. Ryan weighs a whopping four pounds, two ounces. Her eyes closed, a protective covering shields a feeding tube into her mouth.

Told to Grandfather Butts by little Ryan

"I not only graduated from cotton balls, but have gone all the way to diapers and dress. What a sight! I continue to show astonishing improvement. I think it has something to do with TLC. I'm not sure what that means but it might have some reference to "My Taco Loving Caretakers" Anyway, I am living proof that this is the best place in the world for a Preemie to get through the early weeks. I hope the doctors and nurses around here don't get the big head over this, they are hard enough to deal with. I like the poem my grandfather wrote about me.

"Preemie Stands For Premium"

Little Ryan was due into a family known for being late
She said one day, I'll not have anyone ever to wait
I'll start my life by being early
And this little trick will surely
Get me all the attention I could ever need
Make my family stand up and take heed
That I am the main attraction
I sure put that expert staff into action

And now that I'm getting the best of care
I'll just lie here and not go anywhere
They'll still get me home a week or so, before I was due
And then Mommy and Daddy can stop being so blue
Right now it's by I/V that I'm being fed
And my blood is turning a bright pretty red
The biggest thrill pertaining to me
Was the day I had my very first pee

I'll soon be able to have Mommy's milk
Then my skin will become smooth as silk
Mother Moss' Moo Service will make the run
Mommy in her pink shirt, that'll be fun
I'm going to get bigger and stronger each day
Those nine-month brats better stay out of my way
I'll have experience and strength and stamina on 'em
And everyone will know that Preemie means Premium.
"Don Butts"

RYAN REMEMBERS GOING TO SCHOOL AND SPECIAL DAYS

"I remember going to pre-school, it was fun to play with other kids. My parents passed up day-care; I guess I wasn't ready. My Grandmother picked me up sometimes and we would go out to eat. **It is my special day.** *Except for the*

time she forgot and went to the racetrack instead. My Mom and I laughed and laughed, but I never let my grandmother forget again. I always say, "Please, don't go to the racetrack, BB."

High school was fun. I was in a special class with other kids like me. Some had more of a difficult time and some learned easier then me. I learned to be very careful and walk on the sidewalk to get on the school bus by myself. My mom always watched to see if I did it right. I don't see very well but my contacts help. I started wearing thick glasses when I was one year old. The contacts are better. I have a

white stick to guide me. It is harder for me to walk than some of the kids. My left leg and arm are a little lazy. I hear them say it is because of the opposite side of my brain and palsy. I really feel bad for the kids in wheel chairs who

aren't able to walk at all. I am lucky. Some of the kids on my bus need more help than me.

I like to go to St. Mary's now with all my friends. It is an adult day care and I have a best friend, Brianne. I call her Brie. Some times her parents take us to Southeast Christian Church to a class special for us and then out to eat. Sometimes we stay overnight at each other's house. Brie is smarter than me and we like each other a lot.

It is my special day."

When Ryan attended High School, she was a re-stocking Walmart Employee

Ryan and best friend, Brianna Dixon

33

DAVE STONE, SENIOR MINISTER OF SOUTHEAST CHRISTIAN CHURCH

"Southeast's Deaf and Disabilities Ministry seeks to meet the individual needs of adults and children (along with their families) who are physically and mentally challenged. We offer classes and fun events for our folks that provide fellowship and outreach to share the joys and burdens affiliated with the disabled. We also work with Special Olympics to further involve folks with Sports and Fitness. I have a heart for this special group of people as my Uncle Greg had Cerebral Palsy and I so appreciate what we are doing to love on these folks."

"I look forward to going out to eat with my grandparents, "BB" and "Popsie", every other Sunday. I always get turkey and dressing just like my Popsie. All of those out to eat people remember my name and ask about me when I'm not along. Sometimes my cousin, Madison, who is five years old, goes along and we sit in the back seat. I ask Madison a lot of questions and she always talks to me. Our Grandparents laugh at us.

It is my special day.

I still like to go to Grandma Mary's every other Saturday while my Mom works. We study words and she lets me help her cook. Sometimes my Dad comes to lunch.

It is my special day.

I know how special I am because now I have two sets of parents. I have a step-dad, Denny, who lives with me and my mom and takes care of us. He teases me a lot but I know how he really feels. He picks me up at St. Mary's adult day care and we have a date to go out to eat while my mom works until 8:00pm some Fridays. My step-mom, Ellen, is good to me and makes me feel special. I have a stepsister, Elena, who lives with my dad and Ellen. I like to visit on weekends. I like having four parents. Some kids have none and I am sorry for that."

A TRAUMATIC TIME UNFOLDS

This author's untimely alarm

Ryan at 20 years old is awakening in the night crying with headaches. Sometimes screaming and throwing up. With her high tolerance for pain, this is just about as alarming as it gets. With Janet holding her in the back seat of my car while my granddaughter throws up in a pan, I drive quickly to the Doctor's office for an evaluation. My heart is pounding, my mind racing, but no time for panic. I remain composed for my daughter and Granddaughter. A cat scan immediately scheduled to run a shunt series reveals no sign of malfunction. A small hole had been drilled into Ryan's skull during a shunt procedure when she was an infant, a catheter passed into a ventricle of the brain. A valve attached to the catheter controls the flow of fluid keeping the fluid away from the brain. Another catheter tunneled through the chest and neck into the abdominal cavity prevents hydrocephalus, a great enlargement of the head caused by an accumulation of cerebrospinal fluid.

In addition to the scan, Ryan's stomach is x-rayed. The tests are negative. A prescription for migraine headaches is given and I return my family home. At home, Janet is hopeful that the prescription will be effective and her daughter's headaches will subside. However, confidence is short lived, as the medicine lowered Ryan's blood pressure and the headaches returned with vengeance.

Consultation between doctors decided the only recourse is to do an exploratory surgery on Ryan's head. This is a last resort and the outcome unsure. The entire family is devastated. "Please God, don't let us come this far and lose our special child."

Risks for any anesthesia include breathing problems and/or reactions to medications.

Brain surgery risks bleeding, infections and damage to brain tissue. A shunt malfunction can be caused by a person's growth and if all goes well, be corrected by replacing a longer catheter. For Ryan, the diagnosis is yet to be determined.

Several family members gathered in the surgery waiting room at the hospital with thoughts of fears of what may happen. Ryan's parents leave their daughter to the Divine power of God and competent hands of the surgeon. They join the family members in the hospital waiting room in silence as the surgery begins. The grandparents are silent. The aunts, uncles, cousins and other family members wait in prayer mode. The minutes summarize troubled and agonizing reassessment. What can the outcome be?

Finally, the waiting is over. The Doctor emerged with the news; his unwavering expression remains professional and firm. "Ryan's ventricle peritoneal shunt showed a failure to function and was replaced. This was something the x-ray failed to display. She will be just fine."

This was the best of all outcomes supported by a released group sigh of relief. When Ryan awakened in the recovery room, Janet and Steven , looked at their daughter's bandaged head and asked;

"Ryan, how is your head?

Does it hurt?"

"No! The doctor fixed it."

"How did he fix it?"

"He cut it off, fixed it and put it back on."

With her Mom sleeping on a cot beside her, Ryan spent a few days recovering at the hospital and never complained of another headache.

Ryan, following instructions from Dad

RYAN'S AUNT SUSAN REMEMBERS

The year is 1983, the day of Ryan's birth. "Janet, you are always my hero."
I raced to the hospital. It was not a good time in my life, so I thought.
Some of us choose our own fate and unfortunately follow treacherous
paths. It was evening. The hospital was dark. The hall, quiet. I tried to
keep the sound of my shoes to a minimum as I scurried alone down the
corridors. Finally, I approached a hallway with huge glass windows on one
side. Someone was still there, gazing through the glass. I slowed down and
as I eased to the window, I saw, on the other side, such a tiny creature,
alive, exposed in a glass box. Her poor little head was elongated. She was
sleeping, but each breath seemed to be a chore. I wasn't sure where a thing
called "Hope" was, so I prayed. I prayed for baby Ryan and for my sister. I
finished my prayer and looked to see the other figure at the window. Tears
were in my eyes and in the eyes of Steve, Ryan's father. His skin was pale
and you knew inside of him was the fight for his family, and on the outside
of him, a search for hope. Seeing the hurt and fear, I wanted to hug him.
Instead, I froze. Neither of us spoke, but acknowledged with our eyes as we
turned and walked our separate ways. My path was to change that day.

You couldn't see Janet at that time; she had been through so much. I
located a leather couch on the second floor in a waiting area. No one was
around so I curled up and slept the night. I awakened to the morning's
hustle and bustle of nurses carrying trays, some with medical equipment
and all of them moving mechanically to do their jobs, oblivious of me. I
awakened to many things that day. Janet's life was in jeopardy and I had
to come back to the family. Whether I knew or not that I needed them,
they needed me.

Three years later, I'm in Janet's living room and she is teaching me how to
interact with my young niece by using balls. A beach ball size is for balance.

We would roll Ryan over the beach ball gently so she would get the feel of the movement. We rolled the smaller balls to her. Ryan didn't seem to care what you did or who held her as long as someone made her feel secure.

Seven years later, on occasion I would watch Ryan for Janet. One afternoon, Ryan and I were rolling the ball back and forth on the living room carpet. Once in a while the ball I rolled would miss, and hit the coffee table. "Oh man!" I would exclaim, "I'm in trouble." All of a sudden, Ryan laughed at me. She laughed and laughed and kept laughing until she couldn't catch her breath. Her body began to shake all over. "My God," I thought; she was having a seizure and I wouldn't know what to do. I went to pick her up, hugged her and headed for the phone to call 911 and her Mom when Ryan leaned back, looked at me and just giggled. She understood. She understood me. She understood a joke.

Twelve years later, I was talking to Ryan on the phone, which I often do, and of course, she asked me, "What are you doing right now?" "I am eating a doughnut." "Why?"

"Because, your Aunt Susan is a pig." I heard the throaty laughter on the other end of the line. Ryan never forgot that remark and to this day, I am a pig. She tells everyone. I now have an odd and unplanned collection of pigs over a period of ten years. Now that Ryan is 26 years old, I have a pig candy dish, key chains, cookie jars, piggy banks, pigs on shirts, blankets etc. You can ask her who is a pig. It is always, "My aunt Susan." I still like my doughnuts and I love my Ryan.

A CLOUD OF THREAT

Susan Leslie Watson

The year of 2009 began at Baptist East Hospital. I told my husband, M.C. I wanted to be with my sister. I spent the night in a chair at Janet's bedside. She had just undergone one of seven surgeries, most yet to be performed, to save her life. She had contracted a deadly infectious staph infection, during spine surgery. She and her husband traveled to another state for her to have a less invasive surgery to correct a disc problem. The surgery was a success but unfortunately, she was infected with MRSA.

I curled up in the chair, pulled a blanket up to my neck and positioned myself to watch her every move should she awaken and need something. Every once in a while, my sister would turn her head and moan in pain. After one of these moans, I took her hand, held it and whispered, "Janet, you are always my hero." Without opening her eyes she belted out a song Bette Midler had sung.

"You are the wind beneath my wings."

It was to my surprise she heard me as I watched her eyes open to look at me. She smiled and was asleep once more. I started giggling to myself. My baby sister never ceased to amaze me or make me laugh. It was at that moment, I knew she was to be ok. She has to be. Ryan is lost without her Mommy.

THE YOU I KNOW

Sharon Lee

If I were to write a story of what my sister's life should have been, it would sound like I stole it from a Fairy Tale.

"Stunning, popular girl, with the mind and wit to take her anywhere, finds handsome boy, marries and goes to school to pursue her dream of becoming a nurse, has beautiful baby girl and lives happily ever after."

This is not what was in store for Janet. She took quite the detour. Simple mundane life experiences were not her style. After she went into labor, and Ryan was delivered premature, Janet dropped out of school to care for her special daughter. The years took their toll. Janet and her daughter have endured many heartaches and physical challenges. Stories within my Mother's book will inspire you, as well as break your heart. I hope to give you a window to the makeup of Janet's strength and character and how I feel about my sister.

"Words will never show, the you I've come to know"

Words from the song, *"If"*, recorded by Frank Sinatra, put my thoughts and feelings about one of the most courageous women in my life, into prospective. I have always loved my sister and knew she is special. I believe she was never really a little girl, rather a young lady, even at the age of three. Janet possesses qualities, my sister, Susan and I are constantly reminded, do not. As the youngest of the three girls, she has poise, grace, and an undeniable attitude that says, "Don't mess with me". As she entered high school, her qualities brought her much attention and admiration from her classmates, especially the boys. Janet, then and now, has a presence that commands attention. She has endured pain and

1997

sorrow that surpasses the norm and would bring the weaker minded to their demise, and through it all, has kept humor and hope. The premature birth of her daughter presented life changing challenges; Janet kept the same qualities and tenacious attitude she possessed as a child. Janet has raised Ryan to become a loving beautiful soul; she has passed down to her the positive attitude and love of family. Ryan, even with her special needs, has become a strong young lady with the qualities and love of life as her Mother. Last year, during her latest challenge, having contracted MRSA in her spine during surgery, Janet faced another life changing event when she underwent a total of seven

back surgeries within a sixty day period. The first surgery was meant to correct a herniated disc. The following six became a desperate attempt to save her life. I don't question if I could have suffered the same indignities that she has. I could, but it would not be with the courage, determination, and humor that Janet carried through. When her hour was it's darkest and trials the greatest, she elevated herself to another level and shined through. I have always looked up to my younger sister; as a child, she was both lady and diva, as a teenager she was the package, equally gracious, sarcastic, humorous and beautiful. I now admire her courage. When asked how she copes, Janet responds, "I find something every day that makes me smile." Janet has always been my baby sister; she became my friend and now my hero.

"Words will never show, the you I've come to know"

Life didn't go as planned, but the stunning, witty girl that captured everyone's attention and heart did have a beautiful baby girl, she met and married her prince, Denny. They do live happily ever after. I thank God for her every day.

UNPREJUDICED

Children with special needs, no longer looked upon as lost or wasted, are welcome members of a society knowledgeable with a modern educational awareness of facts. The special needs members of our communities are human beings with feelings of compassion and conscious emotion. The sensitivity they feel inside sometimes isolated in a frustrated mind, causes them to respond in a dispiriting manner. They have talents yet to be discovered.

"In 1920, Noble W. Kendrick of Lu Lu Temple in Philadelphia, after visiting the

Home for the Incurables in Philadelphia, encouraged the National Membership through his office of Imperial Potentate to "Inaugurate a movement among the Shriners of North America for rehabilitating orphaned, friendless, crippled children." As Noble Kendrick led the National effort, Dr. Barnett Owen, Medical Doctor of Louisville, KY, a leading orthopedic physician in the State of Kentucky, an active member of the Shrine Temple, and teacher at the medical college, focused on a local effort.

SPECIAL OLYMPICS

Families and Communities, through the years, becoming more aware of the potential capabilities of citizens with special needs, are creating programs designed for training and competitive opportunities such as Special Olympics. Special Olympics, created in 1968 by Eunice Kennedy Shriver, provide training opportunities and sports activities to children and adults like Ryan throughout the world. More than 90 countries are participants. The Joseph P. Kennedy, Jr. Foundation Headquarters of Special Olympics International are in Washington, DC.

Community organizations with a volunteer commitment, dedicate an ineffaceable impression on the families and children whom they support. Every week, at a farm dedicated to making a difference in the health and support of a child's tomorrow, Ryan's mental and spiritual attitude heightens as she learns care and compassion for animals through horse grooming. By sitting upon a horse led around a track by compassionate volunteers, her posture and memory improve to impact self-reliance, and better health, and promises an improved quality of life. "The supporting cast of nature in an outdoor theater of celestial wonderment delivers an expression of gratitude to a favoring audience from the heavens and God".

Therapy with horses has been around for many years and is available throughout the world. Horse Therapy is not only therapeutic for the development of the special needs but teaches children to cope with anti-social skills, behavioral problems and emotional disorders. Therapy with horses is a way to develop self esteem, new skills, and inner strengths. Troubled adults have benefitted by Horse Therapy through interactions with others, with the world, gaining feelings of security and communication, energizing the body and deterring the mind away from current problems.

"Horses have a good sense of smell, sharp ears and keen eyes. Most Horses have good memories and can easily be trained to obey commands." *World Book 2009.*

When Ryan was born, the recommendation by one of her physicians to place her in an institution was quickly denied, and justly so. The prognosis given was that Ryan would neither walk nor talk and become a vegetated burden to her family. "Not this family!" The prayers and undying determinations of her parents and family members, enforced by Ryan's will and effort of control, fueled her natural feelings and ability to achieve beyond belief of reality. Ryan has far surpassed expectations circumscribed by the boundaries of a negative view.

The Luci Center with Aunt Jackie

In earlier times, in an uneducated society, shame felt by family members and mockery by the more fortunate forced children with disabilities to live in institutions under appalling conditions, treated as criminals and shunned by families. Common punishment with restraints hindered the possibility of learning skills or gaining knowledge.

Thanks to opportunities offered by "The Special Olympics" and other organizations, it is heartwarming to watch as children and adults with special needs show pride in applauding themselves, interacting with one another in a great number of sports. The untapped joys and boundless enthusiasms set free by acceptance and dedication of a hopeful society fades restraints of past negative attitudes towards special needs citizens. Desires to foresee a beneficial justification to educate the Special Needs citizens of our world became an optimistic interest of a more hopeful public.

Ryan is enrolled at the Luci Center, a local Therapeutic Riding Center. She attends once every week during seasonal activities. The Center provides training, education and customized attention to each of their clients as well as commitment to the horses, treating them with dignity and the best care possible.

THE LUCI CENTER

"The Luci Center is a non-profit 501c3 organization located in Shelbyville, Kentucky providing therapeutic riding and hippotherapy for individuals with disabilities. The mission of the Luci Center is to enrich minds, bodies and spirits of individuals through horse related activities. Founded in 1997 by Paula Nieto, the current Executive Director, an enriched therapeutic environment is offered to clients from a multi-county area in Kentucky and Southern Indiana. Housed on a 26 acre farm The Luci Center offers volunteers and participants a beautiful, peaceful environment where the unique experience of interaction and learning about horses takes place.

Paula mentions about how Ryan inspires the volunteers as she sings her made up horse riding songs as she is led around the track. She puts a smile on everyone's face as she continues to sing *"On Patton, around the track we go."*

Jackie Irwin, a volunteer at the center, also Ryan's Aunt Jackie, looks forward to Ryan's visits. "She is always such a joy and willing to do what she is asked to do." Jackie exclaimed. "When she finished brushing the horse, she would say",

"Got that done!"

"What are we going to do now?"

"She is always so happy."

With Jackie is knowledge of the center. She initially inspired Ryan's family, to join.

Word of mouth is often the best contact.

Flower Girl

AN UNEXPECTED TRAUMA

An emotional shock affects the family. It is December 2008. My daughter, Janet, suffering from severe back pain, scheduled a laser back surgery in Florida after she was unable to get an earlier appointment with a surgeon in her hometown. Receiving the message from the Spine Institute that she is a good candidate and the center had some down time to fit her in to a tight schedule was a gift from God to Janet and her family. This meant the surgery is going to be less invasive; she would not have to be away from work for an extended time and she would be home to care for her special needs daughter sooner than a more invasive surgery would permit.

The surgery was completed; the extreme debilitating pain she had felt before the surgery has subsided. She is able to walk soon after the surgery and, within a few days, accompanied by her husband, Dennis, arrives home to rally in the success of their decision.

Life is going to be good. Ryan will return home from her dad's in a few days and resume the normalcy to which she has grown accustomed. Ryan, now a 25 year-old special needs adult, is insensitive to diversity of change. Although she responds in numerous ways equal to her peers in her stage of life, her mentality remains challenged.

The prosperity of good fortune is about to become invaded by a condemnation of fate. Janet, home just a few days recovering from a successful spine surgery is taken ill with flu like symptoms. An emotional shock will affect the entire family. On Christmas day, as the family prepares to celebrate a festive yuletide gathering, Dennis prepares to take his wife to the hospital emergency room. The hospital staff, realizing the severity of her condition, immediately notifies a specialist in the field of spine surgery. The diagnosis, made after an MRI, revealed an infection in her disc, the same disc repaired during surgery. MRSA, methicillin-resistant staphylococcus aureus, threatens to invade her body. Statistics suggest that this type of infection kills 90,000 people annually, more than Diabetes, Influenza and Aids.

Surgery scheduled, in the evening hours, to scrape the infection away from the disc and spinal column indicates there is no time to waste. Janet remains in the hospital for a few days before going home, only to suffer the symptoms of reoccurrence of the dreadful infection. Back to the hospital and another surgery, another and another where all fail to destroy this highly drug-resistant infectious disease. Finally, the surgeon collaborates with another team of surgeons, and Janet, transferred by ambulance to another hospital, prepares for additional surgery. A group of surgeons evaluates her condition and decides what procedures are available to give her a fighting chance.

Prayers are coming from around the country and from Europe, from family members, from friends and acquaintances, co-workers and from caring doctors and nurses and church members. Former school friends keep a prayer link on the Internet.

Ryan's world crumbles when her Mother faces a life-threatening crisis. Although her mentality remains challenged, Ryan responds in numerous ways equal to her peers in her stage of life. The inseparable bond with her mother allows sensitivity of fears and insecurities to invade her body. Her eyes well with tears as she continually asks questions in desperation concerning her precious Mommy. In addition to severe pain and sorrow, not ready to face an unbearable outcome, the family is grieving for Ryan as well.

Janet, with a deliberate determination to survive, holds on to a prayer blanket made for her by her boss's wife. Her family and friends keep a vigil at the hospital through all the critical times. Each new surgery gives a new recital of threats; paralysis, another infection and death are clearly dreaded fears. The surgeries are so close together, prayer is the principal reliance of recovery.

Ryan understands that when her Great Grandmother Pearl became ill she could no longer visit the nursing home to see her. When Grandfather Moss became ill, he did not come home. She missed seeing him in his favorite chair looking out the window at grandma's house. She tells of times when she dreams of Daisy, her dog that went to heaven. More recently, her Meemaw became ill and went to live with Jesus. Ryan's world, shattered by her capacity of understanding, is facing serious threats. Her Mommy, whom she depends on daily, is in the hospital unable to sit or stand until yet another surgery is performed to support and restore her weakened body.

Janet is flat on her back and heavily sedated. She looks different. When Ryan visits, the quality of a companionship connection with her mother familiar to Ryan is absent. Ryan's eyes well with tears, her mouth quivers while her body trembles with fear.

Aside from watching my Daughter's fight for life, it is emotionally draining to watch my Granddaughter's world crumble, threatening assurance of her mother's recovery. It is a reminder of how Janet suffered when little Ryan struggled for survival after a premature birth. Ryan asks, "is my Mommy going to take the Big Road?"

RYAN AT ST. MARY'S CENTER

I hear my dad and other people talking sometimes when they think I don't understand. What I understand is that my Mommy is in the hospital and very sick. I miss my Sweetheart Janet. I go to the Chapel everyday at St. Mary's and I ask God to let me have my Cooking Lady Mommy back. It has been a long time since I slept at home at my Mommy's house. My friends at St. Mary's miss my Mommy too. My friend, Brie, prays for my Mommy with me. Brie is sad like me. I have to remember to **concentrate.** *That is a word I learned to help me do things better.*

When my Dad takes me to the hospital to visit, sometimes my Sweetheart Mommy can't sit up and hold me. I don't want to leave but my Janet needs to rest. My Dad, my guitar Guy, tells me everything will be all right and my Mommy will get better. I think he tells me that to help me not be sad. He plays music for me to make me feel better.

GENTLE CARE AND EXTENDED RECOVERY

A combination of prayer and a total of seven surgeries performed within a period of 67 days saved my daughter's life. The tenacity of a group of qualified surgeons having the expertise to enlist the skills and services of one another, working effortlessly, insured superlative treatment to a patient with a dreadful disease. Janet's unrelenting influence to survive the dire effects of an unpropitious infection claims victory, combating the effects of MRSA. The scars on her back and stomach are healing reminders of many surgeries and of the precious importance given to the existence of life. The devastation suffered by Janet, her family and her friends may have been avoided by a careful task of hygiene during the initial spinal column procedure.

NOTEWORTHY REPORT

Re: Precautions to fight Infectious Diseases.

According to a study by Wyeth Pharmaceuticals; "In the United States, hospital-acquired infections in the United States, afflict over two million patients and kill almost 90,000 people annually, more than diabetes or influenza/pneumonia."

Conflicting reports on a decline and/or elevation of staph infections, centers attention on MRSA, methicillin-resistant staphylococcus aureus. The 60% increase in MRSA, a highly drug resistant infection and other infectious diseases since the 1970's, is unconscionable.

This is a community issue. Increased infection control obtained in laboratories by surveillance and screening of patients and health care workers may be a start. Signs placed in public bathrooms throughout our cities may be a much-needed reminder to *"**Please Wash Hands**."*

Where is the accountability?

As a follow up, letters to the Health and Welfare Departments, both Local and National sent by this author and concerned family members urging responsible government to support a new legislation, received responses by our Senator and State Representatives.

In a letter sent by the office of Congressman John Yarmuth, dated May 15, 2009, is the following quote.

*"**You may be interested to know that in the 110th Congress, legislation ws introduced that addressed this issue. H.R. 1174, the Healthy***

Hospitals Act, would have required public reporting of hospital data, and established a pilot program that would provide incentives to hospitals that demonstrate significant reductions in infection rates. While this legislation did not come to the House Floor for a vote before the end of the 110th Congress, please be assured that I will support this legislation should it be reintroduced in the 111th Congress."

Thank you Senator, but what do concerned citizens have to lose before the legislation is reintroduced for a vote in the Congress? Two million cases each year of hospital-acquired infections, life threatening and avoidable, merit immediate correction..

RETURNING HOME

Ryan's visits with her mom are more frequent now. Janet's road to recovery and ability to re-enter a life remembered is lengthy, but the predominant passion to recover extends an invitation of spiritual strength and relentless determination. My daughter and Granddaughter have an unbeatable bond and a dual strength, revealing a lasting continuance of life.

Family members and friends breathe a guarded sigh of relief, exercising a watchful care of concern, feeling sufficient fear, and rendering an eagerness to assist. Janet's family and many friends continually provide a watchful eye and offer a helping hand. As days go by, Ryan spends weekends at home and sleeps in her bed at,

"My Mommy's House".

Rehabilitation continues as the two of them go on short walks together. Ryan holds on to her *"Sweetheart Mommy"* making sure she doesn't fall.

On another occasion when Janet, accompanied by her daughter, visits her surgeon for a post operative check up, Ryan, still unaffected by the intimidation of the many branches of knowledge and authority, blurts out;

"Doctor, you had better not hurt my Mommy.
And, hurry up, my uncle John is waiting in the car."

Ryan's World is returning to the reliable trust and dependence to which she is accustomed. Although her Dad, *"My Guy",* and Ellen, **"My Step Mom",** parents devoted to giving her loving care, Ryan 's awareness of returning to her **"Cooking Lady Mommy"** and **"Step Dad Denny"** is uppermost in her mind.

WHAT IT MEANS TO BE THE MOTHER OF A SPECIAL CHILD

Janet Clifford

It means constant caring. It means nurturing; it means listening to others giving advice or relating comparison stories and noticing curious stares. In Ryan's case, it means listening to questions over and over all her waking hours. It means awareness of the threat of seizures and paralyzing terror during the devastation of critical times. The desire for solitude and privacy is sometimes beyond alarm. It means having the wisdom and understanding to deal with the facts; the recognition of behavioral changes demands a quest for freedom and imagination of normalcy.

It also means looking into the eye of a soul more beautiful than ever imagined. It means a better understanding of oneself and how God has singled you out, knowing you are equipped with the skill and the drive to accept his offer of such a precious gift. God's love shines every day through the heart of my special daughter. Her joy and zest for perfect day is unending. She delights in every small favor. When we go to the grocery, she stops in the aisle and hugs me for buying a simple bottle of tea.

"Thank you Mommy.

Thank You for buying that for me.

It is my favorite".

Her love for music is an inspiration to all the family. She is a reminder to listen, not only to music but to the quiet, and to breathe the fragrance of flowers, to take time out from the tension and pains of reality in matters which cannot change. She reminds us of the love we have for her and for one another and of the importance of calm in a society claiming a world in irreconcilable difference.

Evidence of Ryan's perception of life and/or death is an uncanny enigma. She awakened recently sobbing and telling me she is having a dream about her "Me Maw". Mysteriously, her dream happened on the first anniversary of my step mother's death. My daughter went to work with me that day and had a special day with Mommy.

What is it like to have a special needs child? It is beautiful beyond telling.

Ryan picks up where her world had stopped, returning home after the weeks turned into months since her Mommy became ill. With my granddaughter's normal routine belonging to her once again, she begins to sing. Her body moves to sounds of music coming from the CD, thoughtfully placed in a player by one of her parents. She continues singing the words she remembers to every song, as loudly as she can, her body and mind refusing to tire. Absorbed in a dreamy hypnotic trance; each song she listens to is her favorite.

Ryan's world starts once again. She begins asking, right after breakfast or lunch, "What are we going to eat for dinner?" Her eyes express motivational dives of shooting stars dancing back and forth. Her mind is constantly advancing to another question before the last one is answered. Ryan is loved by all family members and shows affection for each. Her younger cousins are patient and understanding. Ellery, her cousin, six years younger, at an early age taught Ryan the alphabet. Occasionally, Ryan and Madison, her much younger cousin, play school. Ryan obediently listens to her teacher's explanation as six year old Madison reads, improvising words she doesn't know.

Ignoring the disparity in ages, my grandchildren have developed a tender feeling of affection for one another.

All the children show an enormous affection, interest and compassion when they visit. Ryan, through the years, has learned from each, always remembering what happened when they were together the time before. When anyone prepares to leave, she is inquisitive, asking questions until absolutely satisfied with the answer. You don't tell her you're going out to eat without explaining every course of food and most of the time, an answer to;

"How do you make that?"

The weeks turn into months and the months into years as Ryan's cousins develop, graduate, maintain positions in society and lead productive lives. Their interactions stay the same with their sweet, lovable Ryan, who remains happy and continues to bring a smile to their faces, instilling love in their hearts. They are worlds apart and yet, never distant. The cousins are adopted siblings for Ryan in a special family relationship.

Ryan's family are not the only ones whose hearts have been captured by such an amicable, good-natured young lady. Her pleasant, agreeable, sweet natured personality has touched the lives of all who meet her and changed the lives of some. Close friends of her parents visit often, always bringing gifts to Ryan on special days. "The shelves in Ryan's room display many stuffed animals, all rendering movements, voices and conspicuous noises upon command.

Ryan's developmental skills have advanced in many ways becoming to a young lady, while her childish mentality remains at a five year old level. Every day is her special day, making everyone around feel special too.

IN RYAN'S WORDS

"I am a big girl, all grown up now. I get up in the morning, make my bed, dress myself and get ready to go to St Mary's. I like singing the hair drying song when my "Sweetheart Janet" dries my hair. I sing when she dries her hair too. "Dry! Dry! Dry the hair". I like to sing that over and over. I like to sing when I brush my teeth. I always need help to put my contacts in. I can't do that. It is too hard.

I like to stand at the counter in the kitchen and drink coffee in the morning like my "Sweetheart Mother". I listen to everything I hear my Janet and Denny talk about. I listen when they are on the phone and I listen when my grandmother comes over in the morning and drinks coffee waiting to take me to St. Mary's. I like to hear everything they talk about. Sometimes I worry when I hear them say someone is not well. If someone is sick, I pray for them in the chapel at St. Mary's. My "Cooking Lady Janet" cut her fingers in the kitchen when she sliced an onion. I really worried about that. She is much better now. I like to help in the kitchen. I like to get the big bottle of milk out of the refrigerator for my oatmeal. I am strong like Denny, "My Hard Working Man". Denny is my Step Dad. When I go to Grandma Mary's she lets me help in the kitchen. Sometimes my "BB" and I make cakes or cookies. I like to do it all.

"It is my special day"

When my "BB, that's one of my grandmothers, takes me to St. Mary's, we play music in the car and sing. We both wear sunglasses. She tells me I look like "Miss Hollywood". I don't know what that means but I like to hear it.

"It is my special day."

At present, Ryan attends classes at St. Mary's Center five days a week. St. Mary's Center, was founded in 1992 through the efforts of Sister Regina Bevelacqua and Mary Jo Payne, as their mission of love and dedication:

THE MISSION OF ST. MARY'S CENTER

"To create an innovative environment which fosters a positive self-image, resulting in developmentally /mentally disabled adults and teens becoming more independent and productive members of their community; To provide meaningful experiences through expanded relationships, & opportunities for personal educational, and social development; To enhance the overall quality of family life by providing a program for special needs adults and teens, while providing respite opportunities for family members and care-givers."

There were only four students in the first year. With a few books and meager materials to work with, they met in an office on the Campus of Ursuline Academy in Louisville, Kentucky. The Center, through donations from parents, businesses and a caring community, is currently located in Middletown KY, occupying the educational building of a Church, and serving a total 150 families.

"St. Mary's Adult Day Training provides: Computer Interest Skills, Gardening, Photography, Square Dancing, Music, Handbells, (Bells of St. Mary's) Field Trips, WII Games, Special Olympics, Seasonal Sports/Competition."

<u>Vocational Training:</u> *"Vocational training is an important part of St. Mary's program. Examples include folding pizza boxes for Papa John's and assembling and folding newsletters for the EACM." Eastern Area Christian Ministry.*

<u>Sports Activities:</u> *"A vast array of sports activities is provided by St. Mary's/East End*

Independents. Many volunteers help support, train and coach the athletes"

Music & Drama: Musical vibrations reverberate through the halls of St. Mary's. Students are provided with English handbell instruction, Choral music, and rhythmic activities, giving them an opportunity to show their love of music. They also have an opportunity to socialize and enjoy the art of music and dance."

The students go on field trips, retreats, discuss values, spiritual awareness and much more. With the donation of five acres of land, the services of St. Mary's is unlimited as they work toward a vision of expansion in the near future.

Facilities such as St. Mary's Center have provided a safe haven for hope and dignity to individuals with limited skills. Their support and the realization that all people should have an opportunity of self importance, protects people from a society once inclined to institutionalize a person with mental deficiencies such as Down's syndrome with mongoloid features caused by a genetic disease. Thanks to these facilities and to all the special caring people such as Sister Regina and Mary Jo, unselfishly committed to saving the lives of those whose only crimes are being born without perfection. Preventing our special needs from being ridiculed and scorned by an ignorant society are gifts from God through these caregivers.

Ryan enjoys the classes at St. Mary's. She enjoys the field trips and helping to deliver pizza boxes to Papa Johns. This helps keep her and the other students motivated. It gives them a sense of accomplishment and self worth. They are happy working together, calling it "team work". Some students have fewer disadvantages than others, both mentally and physically. All of them express strength of feeling and keenness of desire in their planned assignments. There are no failures at St. Mary's. All of these students have progressed by interactions with one another, through the love of families and by the school's curriculum. It has been said:

"Imperfections are the soul of a beautiful house".

Ryan has advanced in development and progressed further than expected. She enjoys her friends and care-givers! It's obvious, when I take her to the center, that they look forward to seeing her as well. Who is to say what the sands of time can uncover for Ryan or any of her fellow "teammates". They are in a happy, safe environment, learning about a life's journey that would not have been available to them at another moment in time.

Remembering the – *The Song: from Charlottes Web Movie* "How very special are we for just a moment to be part of life's eternal rhyme..." Sister Regina quotes,

"How very special are we for just a moment to be part of St. Mary's in our life time!"

When I visited an opening of one new local department store with Ryan and her ***Mommy,*** a piano player began to entertain shoppers by playing a song that Ryan had heard before. At the piano player's invitation, when she noticed this young special girl singing out loud and moving to the music, Ryan went to the microphone and began to sing as loud as she could. Singing, absorbed in a trance, as if she were in the privacy of her parent's car singing along with her favorite CD's. When the song had ended, a crowd of delighted shoppers, some teary eyed, began to applaud a young girl with obvious vision impairment, mental disabilities and slight palsy on her left side. Ryan rejoiced in her noticeable achievement and began applauding along with them. Walking away and joining us, drifting along with other shoppers, Ryan immediately diverted her thoughts to the next project;

"What are we going to do now?"

Ryan unceasingly shows interest and awareness of external reality, although the scope of her comprehension hinders her complete understanding of many things. Standing with a steady posture, one ear at an angle assuming a readiness command of attention, with her eyes flashing, Ryan continues with questions until completely satisfied with answers or until the endurance of the listener supports a need to create a diversion of attention. She continues to amaze me, identifying our location when taking her places. With limited vision, holding her head down, shielding from the bright sun, she comments as we pass a place familiar to her;

"There is my mommy's work".

Accomplishments achieved by Ryan transcends beyond early expectations and statistics of an early birth. However, prospects are currently limitless, with ongoing medical technology, communities of caring individuals and the affection of loving families, affording many miracles in future times.

My memories of Ryan as a small child, before she could walk at five years old, include my allowing her to take one Kleenex out of the box at a time and tossing them about. When she finished with that she crawled into the bathroom and unrolled the toilet paper from a wall bracket. I was elated at such an achievement. Her mother, on the other hand was less amused. After all, her parents were working diligently, dedicated to teach their special daughter to live in a standard environment, effectively influencing her development by definite structure. I believe it is a grandparent's affectionate sense of duty to stir up a little reign of innocent chaos with a grandchild occasionally. After all, pay back can be a divine justice.

Ryan, age five

In March of 1996, because of changing intensity of a chemical condition affecting the hormonal functioning of Ryan's health, causing internal hemorrhaging, it became necessary for Ryan to endure another surgery. Upon the doctor's advice, a hysterectomy was performed. She was twelve years old. During her recovery and while her parents worked, caring for Ryan became a small task for me. She never complained of pain. She obediently rested on the bed most of the day and, with the exception of one sudden epileptic seizure as I lay beside her, never gave cause for alarm. The successive stages of Ryan's development have been a process of attention well worth the effort of unconditional devotion.

The natural behavior in the freedom from deceit is a quality of humor to look forward to. The honesty of rejection when Ryan is asked,

"Are you tired of me?"

"Do you want me to leave now?"

"Yes!"

You can count on Ryan to tell it the way she feels.

Always at lunch, I ask if I may have a bite of her dessert; her response;

"Yes, it's good to share."

One particular day at lunch, while salivating over her cheesecake and holding my fork closer, I politely asked.

"Ryan, may I have a bite of your dessert?"

Without hesitation and not missing a bite, she answered,

"No"

The unlikely response was so funny that the people around joined me, rocking with laughter. Ryan, still eating her dessert, was oblivious. Ryan likes all foods but seldom overeats. She has turned down treats to save herself for the next scheduled sit down meal and **"Big Food"**

Crowds in a confined area trouble her. If too many people are within her space, talking at once, she is capable of entering a state of agitation and, in tantrum mode, begins to hit herself. It has been explained to me by a health professional that, to Ryan, it is the enormous sound of an approaching train. Her reaction is one over which she has little control. Prepared for a signal, offering awareness of this situation, leads conscious family members to quickly divert her attention and promptly lead her to a quieter place. This usually works as she again becomes calm.

In the world of a special child such as Ryan, there are roads of conquests, pitfalls of mystique, yet joys of accomplishment. She will continue to grow emotionally and spiritually, maintaining the ageless innocence of a child. Ryan will never have a marriage or bear children. She will live with her parents, and in a supervised group home. However, the conditions affecting her development shield her from a world in pain. Through Ryan, we become aware that many things one worries about are of no importance at all. She reminds us how rich and beautiful life is. Her environment protects her, giving her a distinct quality of life. Her unconditional love swells in the hearts of her family and friends. Her positive attitude projects a powerful influence.

As a teenager, Ryan shared a room with her best friend, Brianne, at the Kentucky School for the Blind when the two of them attended a two week summer camp. The two have remained best friends at the St. Mary's Center. Brie's development, advanced in some areas beyond Ryan's, extends a protective maternal instinct toward Ryan. The two families exchange times when the girls spend an overnight with one another. Brie's family, upon occasion, takes Ryan along to accompany them at church functions. The normalcy of their relationship gives credence to the importance of having a best friend.

"A friend should bear his friend's infirmities," (Shakespeare)

The souls, dehumanized, tortured, and lost through the crevices of the evils of ignorance, are forever remembered through the faces of those who have witnessed the pain.

SISTER REGINA'S INSPIRATION

"Please don't forget us." "Are the words of a senior class student, Stacy Gephart, at Ursuline – Pitt School, where Sister Regina was principal for 25 years and Mary Jo, a Montessori teacher for 15 years.

Sister Regina remembers, *"Stacy realized upon graduation many activities and opportunities would not be available to her. She was already missing her active academic and social setting.*

Unfortunately Stacy's life–journey was cut short because of a brain tumor. However, her words of advice echoed relentlessly through our hearts and minds.

We had taught children with special needs long enough to witness so many "Fall between the cracks". Some would face rejection and failure in jobs. Others were employed such few hours that they faced many lonely and unfulfilled hours during a week – sitting at home, watching TV, sleeping and depending on parents/family for their total social life.

St. Mary's Center was created to put energy, enthusiasm, and fun back into the lives of these special citizens 21 and older. Our goal is to provide "quality" day experiences interacting with many others.

When Ryan enrolled at St. Mary's, she brought with her an aura of gentle sweetness, keen awareness and a beautiful singing voice. Because of her talent, Ryan and her Mom were selected to lead a sing-a-long at one of our fundraisers on the Princess Boat. They sang, "I have a Dream" a song from the movie, "Mama Mia" Hardly a dry on the boat during that moment! The words, "I believe in Angels" in the song truly fit the families, staff, donors and friends. We were all on this "Ark full of Angels" – everyone guiding and supporting one another. *What greater gift in life is there? What higher calling?"*

Appreciation and acknowledgement extends to those silent contributors, such as Sister Regina, spoken only in the faces of the families whose lives are changed forever.

Watching Ryan develop mentally and socially for over two decades, disputing the early prognosis of health professionals with a scientific view of logic, has given the family an indelible memory of hope and pride. God's direct intervention, the role of Ryan's determined parents and family members, influenced the touching heart of child longing to become accepted into a world of attachment.

Ryan's childlike humor is unending, leaving treasures of cherished recollections to all who know her. At an earlier age, after assuming knowledge of some of the dangers in a world of technology, Ryan and I were driving alone when I reached for my cell phone to call 911. I discovered that a car had turned over in the medium, with what appeared to be a small child and young woman trapped inside. Ryan's concern about me using the cell phone prompted her to repeatedly and with a demanding voice, instruct;

"It is dangerous to use the cell phone when you are driving"

The traffic accident, that Ryan was oblivious to, was minor. Rescuers came upon the scene and we went on our way. From that day, I am forever remindful of a potential danger from the comment by my granddaughter, once given up to an existence of darkness.

Ryan revels in the excitement of holidays. On Christmas morning, she gets up before dawn, usually to be guided back to her bed by a sleepy parent. When smaller, it was fun taking her out, dressed as a bunny, for "Trick or Treat". Her excitement now, for Halloween, is to hand out treats from the front door. One year, not many children came to the neighborhood. Not wanting to disappoint Ryan's enthusiasm of hearing the doorbell ring and her eagerness to hand out a treat, her mother, donned with a sheet over her head and repeatedly running around the house, from the back to the front door, masqueraded as a Halloween beggar while I remained with my granddaughter. We depended upon

Ryan's visual impairment for this deceit. She soon became convinced all the tricksters went home to bed.

I remember another time, not so commendable. While in my care, Ryan accompanied me to the eye doctor. I had to admit to my daughter that we

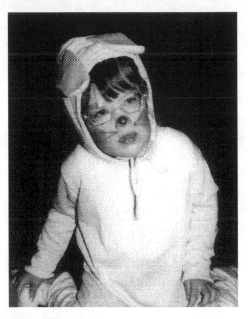

drove home equally handicapped. Unbeknownst to me, eye drops inserted would leave me visually impaired.

"You mean, you drove my daughter after your eyes were dilated?" She asked. "But it was only a few blocks". I replied. Still, not smart!

Ryan has special needs, but has come far and acquired many abilities. Aside from needing help occasionally with cutting up food on her plate, she has full control at every meal. Her morning schedule includes dressing herself every morning and making her bed. She takes great pride in every detail of accomplishment. With the exception of not realizing time spans, things that happened last month she refers to as last week, Ryan's memory is exceptional. You had better not invite her to an event without making good the invitation.

The early prognosis of the quality of Ryan's life, predicted from the facts that Ryan would never walk, never know her family, become blind, etc., is undeniably intervened by the divine powers of God, working through the efforts of a loving family and a child's soul with the determination to deliberate command and control to surpass expectations. When we get into the car, she buckles her seat belt faster than I can buckle mine. Although, legally blind, having to depend on contact lenses, Ryan knows when we approach a familiar destination. She knows left from right and sometimes points things out to me, as she did today, telling me the truck in front of us turned left because he had a green light. Of course she wants to know where everyone on the road is going. When we reached our destination this morning, she was quick to remind me that I goofed by not playing music in the car. I think sometimes she delights in not reminding me so she can tell me, "you are a goofball, you, didn't play the CD." She really gets a kick out of saying that. She also knows her schedule for the week; what day she goes to her Dad's, what day her step-dad picks her up when her Mom works until 8:00pm, and remembers what day it is when she goes to the Luci Center to ride a horse named Patton.

I am proud to take Ryan places. Her personality shines through her remarks of personal distinction. She always answers when spoken to. And above all, she has many questions to ask. All who meet her enjoy conversations with her and the humor revolving from some of her unpredicted remarks. Her happy disposition is infectious. She has special names for family members. Her mom is sometimes called, Mommy, Janet, Sweetheart Angel, Ma, and Cooking Lady and so on. Ryan sometimes calls her dad by his name, Steve or Dad and often, she refers to him as "*My Guy*" and "*Guitar Dude*".

Although she currently lives at home while attending day classes at St. Mary's Center and Apple Patch, Ryan is expected to move into Apple Patch in the near future with frequent, unrestricted visits to her parents' homes.

Apple Patch is a facility developed on donated land to accommodate residents with intellectual and developmental challenges, in Brownsboro, KY. The facility keeps expanding. The newest Apple Patch Community Development will include 76 homes and 42 condominiums. Some of these homes are single family homes and others are group homes. Ryan will live in a group home.

A quote from: applepatch.org

"Apple Patch is an organization dedicated to promoting a life of independence for adults with intellectual and developmental disabilities. We believe that many individuals are capable of independent living, yet have never been given an opportunity to reach their highest potential in an environment where their skills are strengthened through "real life" experiences in the community.

We know that positive, affirming life experiences are the foundation to leading an independent and productive life. To help individuals accomplish this, we will ensure that each person we serve is provided the opportunity to live as independently as possible in an integrated setting...and given the support to make choices among residential options, employment opportunities, social and recreational activities, and skills training to achieve the goals to which they aspire."

*A quote from: **homeoftheinnocents.org***

Mission Statement:
"The Home of the Innocents, a
community of dedicated people
and those they serve, provides
the skills and opportunities by
which vulnerable children,
youth and their families may
improve their lives."

"Home of the Innocents is also
there for children who are
medically fragile, technology
dependent, or terminally ill. Our
Kosair Charities Pediatric
Convalescent Center is this
region's only long- term
residential facility for kid's ages
infant to 21, with physical and/or
developmental disabilities."

When Ryan was three years old, her mother, Janet, became co-chairman
of the Intensive Care Nursery Parents Association. The group, a non-profit
organization incorporated in 1983, provides emotional support to parents
of critically ill infants. When Ryan was born, there was no such support
group. Janet exclaimed, "I don't know if I would have wanted to talk to
anyone at the time of Ryan's birth, but it is nice to have the choice. What
helps many parents, is knowing that this doesn't just happen to them.

After Ryan's 14 week premature birth, she survived an incredible number of medical complications requiring surgery. Some premature babies catch up during the first year of life. However, at 26 weeks gestation, at the time of Ryan's birth and one of the smallest to survive weighing just less than one pound and a half, there were no babies to compare her to. Janet recalls hearing that brain damage is one of the complications. Recalling the ordeal, she exclaimed, "brain damage sticks with you more than you like."

Dealing with barriers is emotional and frustrating. Conquering impassioned defeat is triumphant. Ryan understands more than she can relate to family members or to her inner circle of friends and caretakers. She is a proud young lady, a vital member of our family. We are grateful to have such a loving human being sharing our lives. Ryan breathes inspiration for the passions of life influenced by the praises of God.

All human beings have strength of mind and spirit with the force to think, feel, and a soul determined to exist longer than the human body. With today's resources, given the power to achieve, the story of triumph, hope and faith illuminating the face of every special needs child, is a collective remembrance of importance. Many children and adults with varying challenges have proven abilities beyond devotion to medieval ideas and presumptions in a misguided society.

Ryan is still working on words from the alphabet with Grandma Mary and delights in writing a grocery list. She loves to help in the kitchen by stirring the cake batter or by getting the milk out, putting groceries away, etc. Every small feat is a victory, influential in affecting her self confidence.

Ryan's mom, deciding it is time to replace Daisy, the deceased family dog, brought Lilly home from a shelter. Lilly, a puppy, with Jack Russell genes coupled with dachshund, is a little high strung. However, the puppy seems to respond with a keen sense of awareness when interacting with Ryan, and displays obvious caution. The enthusiasm is limited to licking Ryan's face until she giggles.

"That Lilly is crazy" Ryan exclaims."

"What?" I asked.

"My sister is nuts" she answered.

"Ryan, Lilly is not your sister. She is your dog."

I corrected, not vigorously convincing enough. Although the puppy is adapting to a loving home willing to give her the attention she needs, Ryan's Step-Dad and Mom are watchful of any aggression toward their special child. For now, Ryan and her sister, Lilly, are companions.

Another favorite for Ryan is when her grandfather prepares to take insulin. She reads the meter and relays to him what the indicator displays as his blood level. She gets as close as she can until her nose is a few inches away to see the needle penetrate. Ryan is intrigued by any drop of blood. The only times she is interested in television is during a surgical procedure and, of course, car races and cooking shows. We can't figure out if she would have been a surgeon or race car driver, maybe even another Julia Childs. The importance of her good health, good humor and heart full of love outweighs any aspirations of what could have been.

Sometimes Ryan gets tickled and laughs uncontrollably if a family member has a minor fall, or goofs such as I did when I mentioned out loud to her that I had turned down the wrong street. We have to remind her to stop and breathe. She then replies when she stops shaking,

"I'm ok now, I caught my breath."

This morning I waited at my daughter's home for Ryan to get ready for me to take her to St. Mary's, as her Mom goes to work later.

"BB, My mommy didn't pay attention to me last night. She didn't do it right. It makes me a little bit irritated."

"Why didn't she pay attention to you?"

"She played that talking on the radio and talked on the phone."

"Do you want me to speak to her?"

"Yes, BB, really please".

"I'm sorry Ryan, I won't do that tonight."

Janet replies rolling her eyes around as if Ryan would ever go without attention.

"Please Mommy, really please, don't do that tonight."

As I drove Ryan to St. Mary's, our conversation continued between the song lyrics of "Mule Train" sung by Frankie Layne blaring from the CD and listening to my delightful, "Il Divo" favorites. We both sing the words we know and make up the rest.

"It is our special day."

The subject changes again, as it often does.

"BB, thank you for taking me to lunch yesterday.

I miss that out to eat when I don't go.

Those out to eat people miss me too."

"I know you do, Ryan," I replied.

"I know they miss you too."

I had taken Ryan along with her cousin, six year old Madison, to Piccadilly's after church on Sunday. The children are always greeted by cafeteria personnel who have learned each of their names over the years. After lunch, the two girls joined Janet and her sisters at Grandpa's home, to supervise their Aunts and Ryan's Mom as they decorated their father's house for the Christmas season. We have discovered keeping both girls is easier than keeping one. They entertain one another. Madison spent the afternoon reading to a very attentive Ryan. The day was pleasant and productive for the decorating threesome.

Madison reading to Ryan

On Tuesday, as we continue our short journey to St. Mary's Center, Ryan sings as loud as she can and drowns me out, and then another pause,

"BB" what are you going to do today?"

"Who, me?

"Yes, sweetheart, what are you going to do?"

I usually make up something like, "I have to do paper work." This satisfies her. If I say I'm going to cook or bake a cake or go somewhere she has been before, then the conversation will go on, with me having to make up stories to satisfy the endless questions. As we sit at the red light, I say, "Ryan, where is St. Mary's?" Without looking up, she points to St; Mary's which is several yards across the street. "Ryan's other senses shine through her inabilities of sight when images are out of range. She often relates to land marks within her area of vision.

At St. Mary's, Ryan quickly leads me down the hall. I have to hurry to keep up with her, even though she walks showing favoritism to her left side, having been affected by a stroke and cerebral palsy. She leads me to the back room where she takes a plastic hangar from the rack and hangs her coat. I have to remind myself not to help in doing these small things for her, as she gains more confidence and self reliance by doing things alone. She does not want help in most cases. We say our goodbyes and I become a remnant of a forgotten morning as Ryan eagerly joins her friends, focusing on their day together and a field trip after lunch to the bowling alley.

Ryan has, by all accounts, reached the magnetism of permanency, turning back the numbers of an everlasting age. She is an adult with a child's mind mirroring combination images of her peers and family. She reacts as a reflection, cataloging childlike mannerisms of adulthood. She will be forever five years old in some categories, much older in others as she continues to fill our hearts with the rapture of great joy.

The condition of being deprived of ability, lacking the advantages of discovery, is appalling in this society. No matter the severity of the disability, a human being is entitled to a support action to increase a chance to improve the process of development. The wisdom of a new age based on knowledge and good judgment has carved a prevailing vision of predominant influence for betterment. The current society has worked hard demanding all wrong doing be punished.

With a firmness of purpose, and a resolution to conquer, Ryan's parents have a dedication to their daughter, preparing advantages for care in the future. By trying new things, such as choosing clothes she wishes to wear for the day, making her bed, etc., Ryan has become more self sufficient and amazingly proud of her accomplishments with the power of eagerness to succeed. There are many things she will never achieve, but being treated as a normal grown-up person gives her strength of stability. With the realization that a child becomes what he or she is made to understand, Ryan is taught to make choices, to feel praise and to know right from wrong. She has learned the power of mind outside itself by the five senses, accomplishing abilities to identify locations.

My hope, not just for Ryan, but all the special needs, is that they be given the advantages available in their development, helping them to thrive and flourish with vitality to endure and overcome achievements lessened by malady.

The accomplishments of my granddaughter advance beyond the occupational levels of social acceptance. Her very birth has changed the lives of family and friends, some, by their own admission, from a destructive life style to a possession of control and meaningful significance. The powers of God continue to work in mysterious ways explaining the unexplained; giving credence to a divine authority.

Ignoring the importance of God's love and acceptance shining through the soul of a special needs person merits displeasing consequences. "Every person has worth as a creation of God". Every person is deserving of recognizable significance, without influences of negative suggestions, emphasizing defects.

Sigmund Freud once said:

"The borderline between the normal and abnormal states is indistinct".

Through Ryan, we see pleasures of what we enjoy, and gratifications, frequently lost by greed of wanting more.

A new year, 2010, is beginning with little changes. Ryan's mom is recovering, and waiting to go back to work after her New Years Eve surgical procedure which repaired hernias caused by the many surgeries of the previous year. Ryan spends two days a week at Saint Mary's and three days a week at Apple Patch. Apple Patch is convenient, as the bus delivers her and brings her home. Her first day riding the bus, after so long a time lapsed since her bus riding days to Ballard High, is a new adventure for Ryan. For that reason, her dad followed the bus. After seeing how well adjusted she is, by watching her leave the bus and eagerly enter the building, Steven notified the family that once again, his daughter became confident of one of her many undertakings. Once she does something new, she applauds her ability, and acquires power to think clearly to repeat the same feat, as if another job is programmed into her mind.

Her memory is uncanny about significant events or happenings, although time elements to Ryan are best defined by referring to an appointment or incident, as last week, yesterday and tomorrow. She does understand the days of the week and what is next on the schedule and, if quite a number of days have passed since seeing one of her grandparents or another family member with whom she has frequent contact, she begins to ask by saying,

"It's been a long time since I've seen my Grandma Mary", etc.

Her unique way of getting the message across without asking directly, is defined when asking questions:

"Where are those cookies going?"

This means, to Ryan, "will I take some home"?

Or...**"Are those people going to stay?"**

In other words, "I want them to leave".

Shopping is fun! Ryan's mother has had many experiences, affectionately dragging her inquisitive daughter to shopping malls and grocery stores. Of course, there is always the stop and hug when Janet places something in the grocery cart that Ryan likes. And then, the unexpected, such as asking in a deafening tone, "Ma, are you going to wash that gray out of your hair?" When, of course, buying hair color. Then, there was attention when shopping at Sam's Club. Janet's legally blind daughter could see the many stacked boxes of supplies and furniture stored overhead almost to the ceiling.

"What is all that? #x%* up there?

She questioned, in her, not so quiet, soft spoken tone. She obviously picked up an unfavorable word and put it to a meaningful question. Janet blushed on that one, when several people turned around with tongue in cheek, inconspicuously muffling snickers at the amusing entertainment.

I learned what Ryan thinks is a bad word when I called out,

"Idiot" under my breath of course, to a motorist who cut me off.

"I'm going to tell my mommy.

You said a bad word."

She shouts between giggles."

This was repeated several times until I agreed.

"Yes! Ryan. Idiot is a bad word."

In order to help her control her breathing because she was laughing so hard, I reminded her to:

"Stop, breathe and catch your breath."

I was afraid she would hyperventilate while I was driving the car.

From that day, I was aware of my un-saintly remarks while......

"Driving Miss Ryan".

"Well, most of the time!"

Through Ryan, we are reminded that although the special needs are an assemblage group, brought together by the destiny of fate, each and everyone is an individual with a unique personality. Each has feelings with the energy of power of mind and body to develop at varying levels. Each is a human being, with a distinct spirit and fervor of emotion. Each one profits through his or her inspiration, crediting the open doors of public awareness.

Our family has profited by Ryan's presence. Unconditionally

accepting the gift of life, which has been deprived of ability or power and lacking advantages available to others, has given us awareness of a value of importance. Her laughter raptures delightful sentiments of great joy absorbing our consciousness with overflowing expressions of life. Ryan reminds us of the beauty of an untarnished soul and the quality of nature. She reminds us of the difference between artificial kindness and natural relationships. Above all, Ryan reminds us of conquering a challenge of evidence proclaiming her fate. Through the power of God, her strength and determinate energy claims a fresh portal imposed on the science of medicine.

Our family and friends have united together collectively, not through the depths of sorrow or a sense of failure, but through a unique individual with the freedom from deceit and aversion from harmful behavior. Through Ryan's exemplified wisdom, we continually discover the true values of life's significance.

REMARKABLE RYAN

M.C. Watson

I was enjoying an adult beverage, watching the local news at a favorite watering hole many years ago. A familiar face appeared on the TV screen and I requested more volume, which the bar-keep obliged. Indeed, it was Janet Moss, sister of a former girlfriend, discussing the wonderful work done by Kosair Children's Hospital. Her daughter, weighing less than two pounds, had miraculously survived despite a myriad of handicaps and infirmities. I rushed home to find Janet's telephone number and gave her a call. She explained all that they had been through in the fragile existence of little Ryan and the doctor's prognosis, for no meaningful life, or even life at all.

Fast forward a few years later, I reunited with Janet's sister, Susan, and we were eventually married. Ryan was still plugging away, with frequent visits to the hospital, and more than a few harrowing moments, but she persevered. Her strength of spirit was remarkable, and an inspiration to all around her. My glorious little niece had defied all odds, and changed one's perspective on "meaningful life". It was said by professionals that Ryan's ability to think, speak, see or walk or function at all would be minimal. Boy was she going to prove them wrong, with help from the dogged determination of her parents, Janet and Steve.

Today, twenty some years later, you would not believe your eyes or ears. She walks the walk and talks the talk. And, oh, does she sing! With a sense of humor few possess, her joy for life infects the hardest of souls. Whether it's music, dance, laughter, or the simple pleasure of a good meal, (Can she eat!!!), Ryan embraces it all, and with that embraces us all. "Thank you, Ryan, from the bottom of your Uncle M's heart."

LIFE IS A GIFT

Susan Leslie

Life is a gift! What we do with that gift is a choice. When I saw my beautiful premature niece, she spoke to me. She didn't know it, but I heard her. I knew at that moment my gift of life was being wasted by me. I couldn't wait to touch and hold her little hand and to teach her; teach her, ABC's, teach her not to run in front of a car, not knowing if she would ever run, or walk, but to dream brings hope.

Ryan was already teaching me. Through the voice of a Preemie, I learned to dream. I learned to hope and I learned to change what I was doing in my gift of life. Ryan taught me to sing, even though I can't carry a tune. Today she sings happy songs and it doesn't matter if you can carry a tune. She can and knows the words to countless songs. The words may belong to another tune, but that's the fun of singing Ryan's way.

If you ever think you are nobody, you are always somebody to someone. Five years ago, I was walking with Ryan across a parking lot to a Walgreens when a young woman approached asking, "Are you Aunt Susan?" I was stunned for a moment by the question from a stranger, then without hesitation, Ryan answered, "Yeah, Yeah, she is. The young woman spoke, "Hi Ryan. How are you today?" She then introduced herself to me as one of Ryan's teachers. I have many nieces and nephews,, each one special to me. Now I introduce myself as Aunt Susan. I have become everyone's Aunt Susan. It's ok! Ryan gave that to me.

Because of Ryan's love of music, I took her to an outdoor afternoon concert. My convertible top was down so Ryan asked me to turn the music up so that she could hear well. She picked out a pair of my sunglasses which she wore the entire day. She rocked in the car and clapped and sang to the familiar sounds on the radio. She attracted a lot of smiles from passers by. After parking the car, Ryan and I crossed the street with our lawn chairs. She held on to one of the chairs, saying, "I'll help you, Aunt Susan."

After finding a spot close to the stage where the band could be visible to Ryan, I noticed my friend, Laurie and her handsome son, Anthony. I was excited to see them. Laurie and I had had several conversations about my niece, Ryan, and her son, Anthony. Anthony has autism. When I introduced Ryan to Anthony, she stood there, a little lopsided, holding her limp hand out and blurted out. "Hi, I'm Ryan." At that moment Anthony bursts out in laughter, joined by Ryan's throaty laughter setting the pace for a delightful day.

Ryan stood next to the stage and sang along with the Country Band as if she were part of the group, smiling and dancing underneath her huge dark sunglasses with her shiny dark hair flopping back and forth as if she is part of the show. In each of our hands is a raffle ticket. It came time for the numbers to be called out and I recognized the number on Ryan's ticket that I memorized. "Ryan, you won." "I did?" "Yes, let's go get your prize." I followed her up the steps of the stage as she put her arm out and traded her winning ticket for a CD. She could not have won a better prize. She proudly held tightly to her prize as we packed up our chairs and back to the convertible; back to our drive home with the music on loud, back to other people smiling as we passed by, back to Ryan's mom to show her prize.

It's a beautiful day with many more to come. Ryan has the gift of music and we have the gift of life.

I BLESS EVERY DAY

Janet Clifford

When you have a child as premature as Ryan, your world turns upside down. You grieve for the child you thought you were going to have as you suffer through the heartache of challenges your baby is facing. Ryan has beaten all the odds, amazing the doctors and other professionals along the way. We always knew she is special, but didn't know to what extent until she grew into the wonderful person she has become.

The stages you go through as a parent of a special needs child are scary, overwhelming and fulfilling. First, you think only about protecting your child from the reality of harshness from people she will come in contact with who do not know her for the special person she is. They sometimes try and look the other way or attempt to communicate awkwardly. Some people are wonderful. I have had the privilege of meeting many understanding, accepting and compassionate people. There are some who ridicule. I was always hurt in these instances and worried how it would affect Ryan growing up and becoming aware of the stares and bad imitations of her.

I should not have worried. Ryan knows love and sees it in everyone she meets. When Ryan was born, I felt sorry for myself. As she grew older, I felt sorry for the things she would miss in life. Again, I worried for nothing. Ryan has not missed out on anything. She is a happy young woman who sings her way through each day. She brings joy and amusement to everyone she meets.

Now that I am older, I wish I were more like my beautiful daughter, loving everyone unconditionally and singing my way through life. I bless every day that I have had being Ryan's mother.

It is difficult to know how many Ryan's have impacted and improved lives of family members and friends of families, bringing to them a realization of the mysterious ways in which God completes his plan.

Today is Sunday. After I returned from church, I picked up my Granddaughter Ryan, to go to her favorite restaurant for lunch, Piccadilly's, after which we

went to my home, made cookies and went for a walk before returning her to her Mom.

"It is my special day!"

Ryan and me

A special "Thank You" to Ryan for her uplifting spirit and to her family and friends, whose contributions of personal recollections helped make this book a sense of completeness.

Thanks to Suzanne Bolus, whose advice, proofreading expertise and friendship, supported confidence to the author!

Research Sources and acknowledgements:

Senior Minister, Dave Stone and Southeast Christian Church's
Outlook, Camp Freedom, August 5, 2004

Follow up article in
The Louisville Times, Thursday, January 12, 1984

Norton Hospital/Kosair Children's Hospital
The Kosair Shriners and Kosair Charities

Eunice Kennedy Schriver and Special Olympics

Sister Regina Bevelacqua and The Saint Mary's Center

Steven Moss and his dreams of a safe place for his daughter, leading to his
involvement in the development of Apple Patch

Paula Nieto and "The Luci Center

Home of the Innocents, whose mission statement is:
"The Home of the Innocents, a community of dedicated people and those
they serve, provides the skills and opportunities by which vulnerable
children, youth and their families may improve their lives."

The cover of this book submitted from the
Fall 1983 Volume 8, Number 3 Issue of Interviews
Norton Hospital/Kosair-Children's Hospital

A special tribute to the fond memory of our cousin, "Fuzzy",
Donald Wayne Proctor. 1938-2005

"When I'm Gone"

(Author unknown)

Forget that I've stumbled and blundered
And sometimes fell by the way
Remember I have fought some hard battles
And won, ere the close of the day.

"A Parting Farewell"

To…..

James H. Nelson, Ryan's grandfather whom she fondly calls,
"Popsie", *a supporter of "Ryan's World", and of Ryan, whom he*
adored, passed from this world Memorial Day May 31. 2010.